Thurgood Marshall

Thurgood Marshall

CHAMPION FOR CIVIL RIGHTS

WIL MARA

FRANKLIN WATTS
A Division of Scholastic Inc.
New York Toronto London Auckland Sydney
Mexico City New Delhi Hong Kong
Danbury, Connecticut

For Maxine Baker, Bernard Goodwin, Jon Harris, Matthew Israel, William Kingwood,
Milton Love, Curtis Martin, Chris Redmond, Eileen Robinson, and Mark Riley.

Photographs © 2004: AP/Wide World Photos: cover, 2, 64, 74, 89, 92 top, 94, 104; Archive Photos/Getty Images: 71 (George Tames/New York Times Co.), 52; Corbis Images: 40, 46, 57, 58, 60, 66, 76, 78, 82, 91, 99 (Bettmann), 92 bottom (Yoichi R. Okamoto), 108 (Reuters NewMedia Inc.), 80 (Flip Schulke), 97 (UPI), 32; Corbis Sygma/ Jeffrey Markowitz: 110; General Mills, Inc. via SODA: 50; Getty Images/Mark Wilson: 35; Hulton | Archive/Getty Images: 22; Jay Mallin Photos/Library of Congress: 20; Library of Congress: 26, 44, 84; Library of Congress via SODA: 9; Lyndon Baines Johnson Library/O.J. Rapp: 86; Moorland-Spingarn Research Center, Howard University Archives: 18; Supreme Court of the United States: 68 (Ackad), 102 (Mary Ramsey Clark), back cover, cover background (Franz Jantzen), 6, 12; The Archives of Lincoln University of the Commonwealth of Pennsylvania: 14.

Library of Congress Cataloging-in-Publication Data

Mara, Wil.

Thurgood Marshall : champion for civil rights / by Wil Mara.
    p. cm. — (Great life stories)
   Summary: Discusses the life and work of Thurgood Marshall, a civil rights advocate who later became the first African American Supreme Court justice.

Includes bibliographical references and index.

ISBN 0-531-12058-9

1. Marshall, Thurgood, 1908–1993—Juvenile literature. 2. Judges—United States—Biography—Juvenile literature. 3. Civil rights—United States—Juvenile literature. [1. Marshall, Thurgood, 1908–1993. 2. Lawyers. 3. Judges. 4. African Americans—Biography.] I. Title. II. Series.

KF8745.M34M37 2003
347.73'2634—dc22

2003013348

Printed in the United States of America.
1 2 3 4 5 6 7 8 9 10 R 13 12 11 10 09 08 07 06 05 04

Contents

This is Marshall circa 1909, around the time of his first birthday. The United States was still adhering to the "separate-but-equal" doctrine, stating that African Americans would live separately from whites but share equal freedoms and privileges. They rarely did.

ONE

Early Years

Thurgood Marshall was born in Baltimore, Maryland, on July 2, 1908. He was named after his father's father, Thoroughgood Marshall, and went by "Thoroughgood" until he decided it was easier to write "Thurgood."

He and his older brother, William Aubrey, were only the second generation of Marshalls born in Baltimore. Thurgood's paternal grandfather, a former slave, fought in the Civil War and settled in Baltimore after the war. He got married and opened a grocery store. He and his wife Annie, had seven children, including a son they named William. Thurgood's maternal grandfather, Isaiah, also fought in the Civil War, settled in Baltimore when the war was over, and opened a grocery store. He and his wife, Mary, had six children, including a daughter they named Norma. All of Thurgood's grandparents were born in the United States, and all were of African heritage.

William and Norma grew up together, went to the same school, and became close friends. They got married in 1905. Soon the couple had their first child, William Aubrey Marshall. Then, in 1908, the young couple had their second son, Thurgood. At the time, Norma was an elementary school teacher, and William worked as a waiter on a train that ran between New York City and Washington, D.C.

SOMETHING OF A WILD CHILD

Early in his life, Thurgood was a quiet, almost meek child. But that changed around the age of five or six. He became more outspoken, bolder, and more willing to offer an opinion on just about everything. Friends and family say he was a relatively happy little boy who loved to smile and laugh. But he also had a serious side, often becoming lost in

Slavery in the United States

Slavery in the United States lasted from the early 1600s until 1865, when it was outlawed by the the Thirteenth Amendment to the Constitution. Slave labor was were used mostly on farms, where it was used to grow crops such as cotton, tobacco, and sugar. Most slaves came from Africa and were often kidnapped, shipped across the ocean by boat, and sold like animals at auction. They were often treated brutally by their owners.

his thoughts. He spent hours turning over ideas in his mind, and he could be very sensitive about certain things.

Another part of Thurgood's youthful personality was a fearless streak that occasionally got him into trouble. He was always ready to fight and sometimes didn't know when it was best to keep his mouth shut. In a strange way, however, this may have put him on the road to becoming one of the most important lawyers in U.S. history. At his elementary school, the principal would often send troublemakers to the basement with a copy of the Constitution of the United States. He told them they had to read and memorize at least one passage from it.

The Constitution was drafted in 1787 when the United States was a new nation. It established a set of basic laws and rules that all U.S. citizens had to obey. It also provided laws and rules that protected citizens from the dangers of a cruel and oppressive government. This part of the Constitution was called the Bill of Rights.

The Constitution of the United States affirms the laws and rules that govern the country. It was drawn up in Philadelphia in 1787 and ratified one year later. A young Thurgood Marshall found it utterly fascinating.

The Bill of Rights was created by the colonists who first came to North America from England in the 1600s and 1700s. These people were treated cruelly by the English government, so they decided to write a set of rules that protected them from further cruelty from any future governments they chose to set up. Each of the ten rules that makes up the Bill of Rights is known as an amendment.

Thurgood, who found himself in the school basement rather frequently, was fascinated by the Constitution, and it wasn't long before he was asking questions about it. His father encouraged this interest. William Marshall had made a hobby out of the law. In his free time, he would visit local courtrooms where legal cases were being heard. He would sit quietly in the back, among the other visitors, and would watch the exciting events unfold. Soon, he was taking young Thurgood with him. It was during these courtroom visits, Thurgood would say later, that he made his decision to become a lawyer. "Before I left school I knew the entire Constitution by heart," he once told a reporter.

A Nation at War

From 1914 to 1918, more than a dozen countries, including France, Italy, Germany, and Japan, became embroiled in what was called "The Great War," which later became known as World War I. Most of the fighting occurred in Europe. The United States entered the conflict in 1917, concerned by a possible alliance between Germany and Mexico and the sinking of U.S. ships by German submarines.

Interestingly, Thurgood's mother did not plan for her son to pursue a career in law. She wanted him to become a dentist, instead. She felt that, being African American, he would have a better chance of succeeding in society if he went into one of the medical professions. Thurgood's brother, Aubrey, would follow his mother's advice and, one day, become a surgeon. But Thurgood, in spite of his love for his mother, would not be swayed. He had found his passion and planned to follow it.

It was around this time that Thurgood also made a painful discovery about the world in which he lived—African Americans were often treated very poorly. Some people would look down on them as if they were lowly and second-rate citizens. Thurgood heard African Americans referred to as "niggers." "Nigger" was the worst thing anyone could call an African American. When Thurgood heard it, he went home and told his father. He said he was angered by it but unsure how to react. His father then told him something he would never forget—"Anyone calls you nigger, you not only got my permission to fight him, you got my orders to fight him." This would motivate Thurgood, especially in his legal career, for the rest of his life.

Thurgood also figured out at a young age that African Americans were often kept apart from white people in U.S. society. For example, in Thurgood's elementary school, there were no white children. Although there were white families in Baltimore, the white students went to different schools. Thurgood noticed that the average school for white children was a lot nicer than his school. It had better books and better facilities. Thurgood also realized almost every family in his neighborhood was, like his, African American. Whites, on the other hand, lived in different areas. So, although whites and African Americans lived in the same

Erupting Racial Tensions

Because of the poor treatment of African Americans, the United States experienced many instances of racial conflicts. In Chicago, after a young African American boy drowned in 1919, rioting between African Americans and whites erupted in that city. The boy had been swimming in an area of Lake Michigan that was designated for whites only. A young white male threw rocks at the boy and struck him on the head. When police arrived, they refused to arrest the person who threw the rocks and arrested a black youth instead. The riots lasted for five straight days, and thirty-eight people were killed.

town or city, they seemed to be living in separate worlds. Perhaps young Thurgood didn't know it at the time, but this practice of keeping the races apart was called segregation, and it was being done on purpose.

Because Thurgood already had such a keen interest in the law in these early years of his life, there is little doubt that he took particular notice of the Constitution's Fourteenth Amendment. It promised, among other things, that all citizens of the United States, regardless of their race, were guaranteed the same civil rights and civil liberties. That meant all citizens of the United States were to be treated

During his years at Frederick Douglass High School, it was clear that Marshall was destined to be a great lawyer. He was captain of the school's debating team. Popular with his classmates, he was also on the student council.

equally and given the same privileges. Because the schools where he and his friends went were definitely not equal to those of white students, Thurgood no doubt felt cheated. What he saw in his world and what was stated in the Constitution's Fourteenth Amendment seemed to be two very different things.

Thurgood finished high school in 1925 and was eager to move on to college. At first, he wasn't sure which one to attend, but he eventually settled on Lincoln University in Chester, Pennsylvania. Lincoln was one of the oldest colleges for African Americans in the United States, and it offered them the best chance of receiving a decent education. Lincoln was regularly graduating people who went on to become doctors, lawyers, scientists, and members of other respectable professions. In fact, Thurgood's older brother, Aubrey, had graduated from Lincoln a few years earlier. On the other hand, however, Lincoln was also a stark reminder of segregation. Educational segregation would become the focal point of Thurgood's anger for many years to come. But at that point, he had to earn his degrees.

THURGOOD GOES TO COLLEGE

Thurgood had worked during the summers of his high school years in order to save up the money he needed to attend college, but when he was ready to go, he still didn't have quite enough. To help out, his mother sold her engagement ring in order to cover the difference.

In his early years at Lincoln, Thurgood continued getting into trouble. He played pranks on other students and often stayed up all night drinking and playing cards, instead of studying. But after he began to feel guilty after his mother had made such a huge sacrifice, he got on track and focused on his studies. He became a good student, earning good grades. He loved to learn new things and played an active role in his classes.

Marshall (second row and second from the right) is shown here with his fraternity at Lincoln University. Lincoln was founded in 1854 and, at that time, admitted only African American students. Today, it is open to students of all races.

Although most of Thurgood's teachers were white and had been trained in exclusive schools, they were also liberal and open-minded, intent on making sure African American students who were eager to make something of themselves got the best education possible. One subject Thurgood and his fellow students spent a lot of time discussing with these teachers was discrimination. Discrimination is the practice of treating a person differently because of his or her race, color, gender, religion, or other difference. At Lincoln, the type of discrimination being discussed was that against African Americans. These discussions, which often became heated and stretched into the night, would fuel Thurgood's desire to *do* something about the problem—to find some way to fight it rather than to simply accept it.

During his later years at Lincoln University, Thurgood would experience discrimination firsthand. One night, he and a group of fellow students went to a local movie theater. After they received their tickets, they were told they had to sit up in the balcony. The seats on the floor, which were the best, were reserved for whites. Thurgood's anger toward discrimination and his desire to fight it grew even stronger.

Thurgood had many positive experiences at Lincoln. He met and fell in love with a young girl named Vivian Burey, known among her closest friends as "Buster." Burey was also a Lincoln student. Although she and Thurgood were both hardworking and dedicated to their studies, they managed to squeeze in dates here and there. They got married in September of 1929, before either of them had finished their schooling. Their parents had reservations about this, but the young couple vowed to stick together and make it work.

Thurgood's growing talent in the area of open debate also became evident while he was a student at Lincoln. With aspirations of becoming a lawyer, he knew his debating skills would have to be razor sharp if he wanted to be successful. He joined Lincoln's debate team, and soon he was its star member. His team was often pitted against those from colleges with longer histories, better credentials, and more money. Regardless, Thurgood led Lincoln to stunning, often overwhelming, victories. He could be vicious and cunning, swiftly spotting weaknesses in his opponents' arguments and using them to his advantage.

Law School Days

Marshall graduated from Lincoln University in June of 1930 with honors. From there he and his wife moved to Baltimore to live with his parents, who had offered their home when Marshall decided that he wanted to go to law school. His parents knew he'd need to save every penny he could. Law school presented many great opportunities. Lawyers held real power in U.S. society, and many of them made a good living, but going to law school wasn't cheap. Marshall would have to work harder than ever, but he was ready for the challenge.

It was at this turning point in his life that Marshall would once again face discrimination, and once again, the ugliness of the experience only served to strengthen his desire to fight it rather than accept it. Because he was born and raised in Maryland, it seemed logical to him to attend the law school at the University of Maryland. It had excellent facilities and first-rate teachers, and he wanted to make sure he got the best training available.

After he submitted his application, however, he learned that the school did not permit African Americans to attend, according to the biography, *Thurgood Marshall: Warrior at the Bar, Rebel on the Bench*. It was segregation, plain and simple. Marshall was understandably angry, not to mention disappointed, and silently vowed to get his revenge one day. He would not simply forget about the injustice.

Marshall applied to the law school at Howard University, which accepted him right away. Howard University was located in Washington, D.C. It was opened in 1867 and, back then, provided education for former slaves. Through the years, it built up its credentials and expanded its course offerings, eventually becoming one of the finest schools for African Americans in the country.

Marshall attended the law school of Howard University, where he became involved in the National Association for the Advancement of Colored People (NAACP).

The workload at Lincoln was tough, but it was nothing compared to the one he endured at Howard. He got up every day before sunrise, traveled from Baltimore to Washington by train, attended classes until midafternoon, went back home to put in a few hours at various part-time jobs, and then studied late into the night. He studied on weekends, too, absorbing every word in every law book he could get his hands on. "When I was in law school, in my first year, I lost thirty pounds solely from work," he once said. Some first-year students quit to seek an easier profession, but not Thurgood Marshall. Shortly after he began going to Howard, he stated that he was certain he wanted to devote the rest of his life to legal work. He was happier than ever.

THE MAN WHO CHANGED MARSHALL'S LIFE

Aside from getting the chance to earn a law degree, Marshall also met someone at Howard who would change his life. His name was Charles Hamilton Houston. Houston was a superb lawyer who had graduated from Amherst College and had also received degrees from Harvard University, one of the most respected schools in the world. Houston eventually became a teacher at Howard. He also worked at his father's law firm, which, like the university, was located in Washington, D.C.

Houston started his career at Howard at a time when the people who ran the college were trying to make it not only the best law school for African Americans but also one of the best law schools overall. That meant the school had to maintain high academic standards. Houston, who loved this idea, was hard on his students, pushing them to learn as much as they could. Many would transfer out of his class so they could get into classes taught by less-demanding teachers. Thurgood Marshall, however, had no such intentions. He knew that Houston would show him how to be the best lawyer possible.

Interestingly, Marshall would say later in his life that he didn't particularly like Houston at first but grew to respect and admire him. Houston could be difficult to deal with, but he was also fair and honest. He would do everything he could to help a student who was really trying. And Houston knew that an African American lawyer would sometimes struggle in court simply because of the color of his skin. He told his students they had to earn every victory on the basis of their legal skills, so those skills had better be sharp.

Houston also taught his students that they should not go into the world to be only lawyers. They should also strive to become something he called "social engineers." Houston thought each student had to fight for the kind of changes in society that would give all African Americans

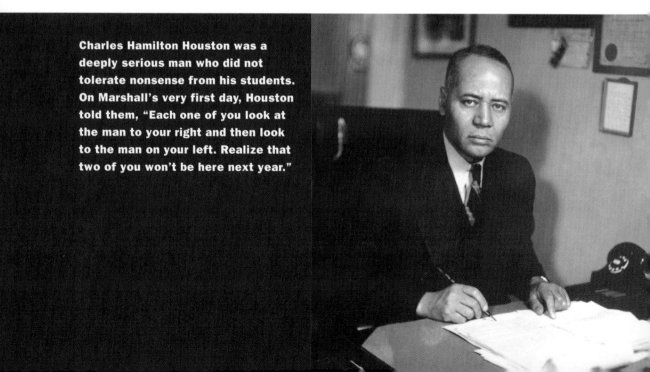

Charles Hamilton Houston was a deeply serious man who did not tolerate nonsense from his students. On Marshall's very first day, Houston told them, "Each one of you look at the man to your right and then look to the man on your left. Realize that two of you won't be here next year."

a chance for a better life. They couldn't just become lawyers because they hoped to make a lot of money. It was their duty to fight for the millions of African Americans who weren't lawyers and who therefore needed people to fight for them. For Thurgood Marshall, who had already seen his share of discrimination, this was a brilliant idea.

Inspired by Houston and by the thought of someday earning a coveted law degree, Marshall worked very hard. He let nothing stand in his way or distract him. He was an outstanding student and, in his freshman year in 1930, was given a job in the school's law library. This job offered Marshall several golden opportunities. Because it was a paying job that would cover some of his school costs, it meant he would no longer have to waste time working all those other part-time jobs, which held no interest for him. Perhaps more important, it gave him the chance to spend more time with Houston and other influential people at Howard.

THE ORGANIZATION THAT CHANGED HIS LIFE

Many of the people Marshall became friends with as a result of this library job were members of an organization called the National Association for the Advancement of Colored People (NAACP). The NAACP was one of many organizations devoted to wiping out discrimination against African Americans. It had a large national membership and had made great progress since it was founded in 1909. Thousands of talented African Americans gave their time and effort freely to aid the organization's cause.

Charles Hamilton Houston was one of those people, and he and many of his lawyer friends, who were also NAACP members, spent countless hours in the Howard law library working on discrimination cases. In that respect, Howard was not only a school for up-and-coming African American lawyers, it was also something of a legal workshop for the NAACP. Many of the legal theories the organization's lawyers used in their important cases were formed at Howard. And because so many NAACP–associated lawyers went to the Howard library, it wasn't long before they took notice of the bright young student named Thurgood Marshall.

There were times when Marshall did little more than sharpen pencils or fill coffee cups. But there were other times when he actually took part in research efforts and even helped write documents that would be used in court. Some said his work, even at this early stage in his career, was better than that of lawyers who'd been practicing for years.

This is an NAACP march to protest lynching laws. The NAACP was formed in 1909, inspired partially by a movement by whites in Abraham Lincoln's hometown of Springfield, Illinois to remove all African-American residents.

Marshall continued pushing himself to the limit at Howard, staying up late every night and sacrificing weekends in order to further his studies. He still spent time with his wife, Vivian, and the rest of his family, but he did little else that didn't involve legal work. All this hard work paid off when he graduated first in his class in 1933. That same year, Charles Hamilton Houston became the leader of the NAACP's legal counsel. That meant he would have the final word on all of the organization's future cases and actions. He decided where the NAACP would focus its energies in the ongoing fight against discrimination, and he said it would be in the U.S. public education system. In order to do this, however, he would need plenty of bright, young African American lawyers to help. Thurgood Marshall was at the top of his list of candidates.

The NAACP and "The Call"

The NAACP began in 1909 as the National Negro Committee. On February 12 of that year, a group of New York citizens put out what they termed "The Call." It was a "battle cry" to fight for justice and liberty for people of all races. The organization often brought this fight into U.S. courts. There were many cruel laws and rules at the time that made life difficult for African Americans. One in Louisiana, for example, stated that white people who were selling their homes could not do so to African Americans.

THREE

Thurgood Marshall, Attorney-at-Law

Before any law school graduate can become a lawyer, he or she first has to pass a very difficult test called the bar exam. The bar exam is a state test that determines whether that person is ready and able to practice law. It is not easy. Many people have lost the chance to become a lawyer because they couldn't pass the test. Others failed it on the first try but passed it on the third or fourth. Happily for Thurgood Marshall, this was not an issue. He passed it the first time. After that, at long last, he was a bona fide lawyer, ready for his first client.

Attorney-at-law Thurgood Marshall, on the left, walks with a client in 1935. Upon graduating from law school two years earlier, Marshall was offered a chance to continue his legal education at Harvard, perhaps the most prestigious college in the world. He chose, instead, to open his own law firm back in Baltimore.

A POOR LAWYER?

Marshall opened an office in downtown Baltimore. There is little doubt he hoped dozens and dozens of people would come streaming in, giving him loads of work. It didn't quite turn out that way, however. In fact, there were long stretches during which he had no business at all and had to borrow money to pay his secretary and his rent.

Eventually, however, the customers came. He became popular in the area because he never turned away anyone who truly needed help, even those who couldn't afford to pay him. He became known as a lawyer who was interested more in helping people than in simply making money. He accepted clients that other lawyers had turned down.

A woman named Lillie Jackson took notice of Marshall's good-heartedness. She was the president of the Baltimore branch of the NAACP. She was considered to be as tough as a bull and as mean as a rattlesnake. According to the book *Thurgood Marshall: Warrior at the Bar, Rebel on the Bench*, Theodore McKeldin, while governor of Maryland, once said of Jackon's formidable ability to push and persuade others, "I'd rather have the devil after me than Lillie Jackson." She cared passionately about the plight of African Americans and hated discrimination with every ounce of her soul.

When Jackson first took over the Baltimore branch of the NAACP, it was a mess. The founders of the organization wanted African Americans to think of it as a group that would make their lives better and fight for their rights. But many African Americans in Baltimore had lost faith in the organization. They felt it had become an organization that helped only African Americans who had money or power. Its members were considered the African American upper class. After Jackson took over as president of the Baltimore branch, she decided to change this perception, and she wanted Thurgood Marshall's help. She wanted *all* African Americans in Baltimore to believe in the NAACP again.

In many ways, Marshall was exactly the type of person that many impoverished African Americans didn't like—he had a solid career, some money, great ambition, and a chance to go far in life. He seemed to represent everything that had caused them to lose faith in the Baltimore NAACP. It would be easy for him to join that elite class if he wished. But he didn't. Instead, he spent time with the struggling families. He visited their homes, where he would often stay with them for dinner or a few drinks. In time, the people discovered that Marshall was truly one of their own. He knew what it was like to go without food, to live in a run-down house with no hot water and rats in the cellar, and to feel the sting of discrimination. Yes, he had risen above the hardship, but under that lawyer's suit, he was one of them.

THE YOUNG CIVIL RIGHTS ACTIVIST

Because he was a lawyer, Marshall decided that the best way to help African Americans was through legal means. He kept his eyes and ears open for cases that would make a difference in the Baltimore community. One of the first involved a string of stores that would not hire African Americans. All the money that was pouring into these stores came from the pockets of African Americans, but the owners, who were white, would only hire other whites.

Marshall sent the word around the neighborhood that these stores should be boycotted. That meant the people of the neighborhood shouldn't go there to buy anything. Marshall hoped the loss of business would make the owners change their minds about hiring African Americans. Instead, the owners became angry and decided to take legal action against Marshall and the others who were involved. They couldn't have made a bigger mistake. The court case was a challenge Marshall was more than happy to take on.

With the help of his friend and former teacher, Charles Hamilton Houston, Marshall argued in court that the people of Baltimore could shop anywhere they wished. If they chose not to shop in a group of stores because those stores wouldn't hire African Americans, nobody could force them to. The judge agreed with him, and he won the case. It was one of his first major victories, not only as a lawyer but also as one of Houston's social engineers. The African American people of Baltimore were thrilled. All of a sudden, they felt they had a real friend in Thurgood Marshall. He had proven himself.

Additional exciting cases soon followed. In one, Marshall successfully forced a number of Baltimore golfing clubs that were for whites only to permit African Americans to play on their courses. In another, he got a school system to give African American teachers the same pay that was being given to white teachers. Previously, the African American teachers were receiving much less pay, even though they were just as qualified and had the same workload. Marshall and his friends also kept up on what was happening at the local police departments. If an African American had been treated unfairly, there was little doubt Marshall would do something about it.

His reputation as a true ally of African American people spread like fire in a hayfield, and soon Marshall was getting more work than he could handle. Some of this work was from wealthier clients who could pay his fees in full. He had put the plight of the poor before the desire to make money, but in the end, the money came too. He was proud of what he had accomplished so far—proud and happy for the people whose lives he had improved.

Something still nagged at him, however—something deep inside that he just couldn't forget. Now that he was a lawyer with a reputation and a little experience under his belt, it was time to do something about it. According to Davis and Clark's *Thurgood Marshall: Warrior at the Bar, Rebel on the Bench*, he was still determined to do something about being turned down by the University of Maryland when he applied to its law school. He knew the reason why. He was African American. He had been an honor student at Lincoln, and he had worked hard and applied himself to his studies. He was certainly as smart as any of the white students who had been accepted, and he was probably smarter than many. So the school really had no good excuse for not letting him in. Once again they were practicing the racist belief of segregation.

Marshall was fair-minded enough to understand that there were some people at the university who didn't like the policy of segregation. It wasn't as if the entire University of Maryland staff hated African Americans. The real problem was that turning down African American students had simply become a habit that no one questioned. Marshall decided it was time to change that.

FOUR

The First Big Cases

Because it had been so long since he had been turned down, Marshall couldn't sue the University of Maryland himself. He had to find someone who was having the same problem that Marshall had back then. In 1934, he found a man named Donald Murray. Murray was, like Marshall had been, an excellent student in college. He had worked hard and had graduated with honors. Because he was born and raised in Maryland, he also wanted to go to law school at the state university. And he also was turned down simply because of the color of his skin.

When Murray wrote a letter to the school's president asking for information on admission, the president wrote back that the school did

Marshall, Donald Gaines Murray, and Charles Hamilton Houston (from left to right) were the three men who successfully forced the University of Maryland to open its doors to African American students. It also made Marshall something of a folk hero within the African American community.

The Troublesome Thirties

The 1930s were unhappy for the average U.S. citizen. Many people had no jobs and found it difficult simply to feed themselves and their children. Because they had so little money, they had to find inexpensive ways to have fun. Some listened to baseball games on the radio. Others began collecting stamps. The famous board game Monopoly was introduced and became very popular. The government launched many new programs to help poor people.

not accept African American students, according to *Thurgood Marshall: Warrior at the Bar, Rebel on the Bench*. Instead, the president said, Murray was welcome to apply to a place called the Princess Anne Academy. Princess Anne was an out-of-state law school for African Americans sponsored by the University of Maryland. African American students who lived in Maryland could go there on a scholarship, which meant either part or all of their expenses would be covered. But Donald Murray didn't want that. He planned to be a lawyer in Maryland, so he wanted to go to law school at the University of Maryland.

The people who ran the University of Maryland were trying to use what was called the "separate-but-equal" rule. The idea was that African Americans were allowed to have everything whites had but that they were to be kept apart from whites. They could shop in stores that were just as good, buy clothes that were just as good, eat in restaurants that were just as good, and so on, as long as they did these things in different places than whites did them. So in Murray's case, the assumption was that the Princess Anne school offered an education that was as high in quality as that of the University of Maryland.

Marshall sued the University of Maryland immediately. One of the strongest points in his case was the fact that the Princess Anne Academy did not offer the same level of education that the University of Maryland did. There were fewer teachers, smaller facilities, and fewer funds. In short, Princess Anne was not even close, in terms of quality, to the law school at the University of Maryland.

Furthermore, Marshall argued, it was just plain wrong to deny Murray admission to the school simply because of his race. Earlier in the trial, the president of the University of Maryland admitted that Murray had been turned down only for this reason. It wasn't so much because he felt any personal hatred toward African Americans. Discrimination had simply become a normal procedure that no one ever questioned.

Thurgood Marshall questioned the policy and, thankfully, so did the judge who presided over the trial. When it was over, in 1935, the judge agreed with Marshall and ordered that the University of Maryland admit Donald Murray to its law school. This turned out to be one of the biggest and most important legal victories for African Americans nationwide.

After the trial, Marshall, Murray, and dozens of others got together for a huge celebration. Marshall was thrilled by the victory on a personal level too. The University of Maryland had turned him down all those years before, and now, at last, he got his revenge.

A STRANGE APPROACH, BUT THE RIGHT ONE

Surprisingly, he and Charles Hamilton Houston were disappointed, in some ways, with the verdict. Their ultimate goal was to wipe out discrimination in the education system throughout the entire country, not just at the law school of the University of Maryland. If they had lost the case, they could have taken it to the United States Supreme Court and perhaps changed the law for the whole country. So, in that sense, they felt they had been denied an opportunity. The Supreme Court, the most powerful court in the United States, makes the final decision on the most important legal matters. Many of the court's decisions have resulted in changes in the nation's laws. The court consists of nine judges, called justices. A decision is reached when five of the nine—the majority—agree on an issue.

Marshall and Houston weren't discouraged, however; they knew there would be other such cases. They went out in search of them. Sure enough, later that same year, one turned up. The pair traveled to Missouri

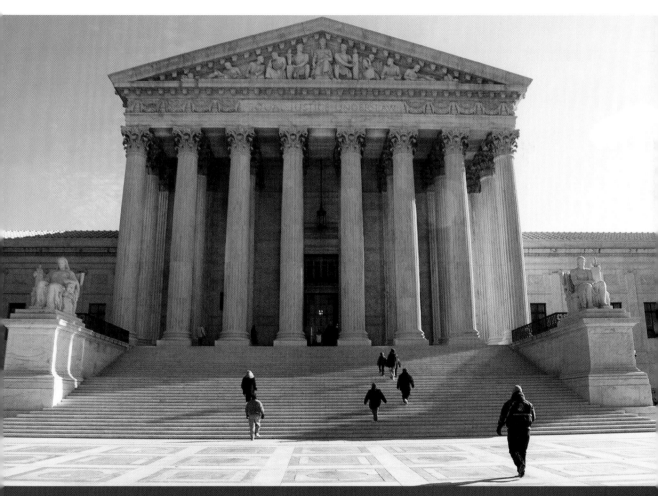

The United States Supreme Court Building is located in Washington, D.C. The president of the United States nominates all Supreme Court justices, but they must first gain approval from the Senate before taking a seat on the bench. There are nine judges on the Supreme Court.

to fight for a man named Lloyd Gaines. Gaines was a Missouri resident who wanted to go to the law school at the University of Missouri. But, just like Donald Murray in Maryland, he was turned down because of his race.

It would be easy to think this case would be a carbon copy of the one in Maryland, but there were a few differences. For one, many of the out-of-state law schools to which Missouri sent its African American students were quite good. They had top-notch teachers and excellent facilities. Also, Missouri was willing to build a separate law school within the state to assure that African Americans were kept separate from whites. The state's lawmakers felt strongly about keeping the two races apart.

In the end, Marshall lost the case, which was exactly what he and Houston wanted. As soon as the case was over, they appealed the verdict so that it would be brought to the next level—the U.S. Supreme Court.

Segregation in Plain Sight

In the 1930s in the United States, even though the NAACP had been up and running for more than two decades and more people than ever before were fighting for the fair treatment of African Americans, there were still many of signs of racial discrimination. It was not unusual for a person walking down the street of a southern U.S. city to see signs like "FOR WHITE CUSTOMERS ONLY" or "SERVICE FOR COLORED CITIZENS AROUND BACK." African Americans had to be careful where they went to the bathroom and which fountain they drank from. If they trespassed on an area designated for whites only, they could get into serious trouble.

When a lawyer loses a case but still feels he or she is right, the lawyer can appeal the judge's decision. That means the case can then be reviewed by a higher court, or a court that has greater power. The higher court might agree with the lower court, or it might decide the lower court was wrong. If that happens, the lawyer would win the case after all.

In this appeal, which began in court in November of 1938, Houston argued that if the state of Missouri wanted to keep African American law students separate from white law students, they should have already built a law school for African Americans within the state. Because they hadn't, it was their obligation to allow African American students to attend whatever law schools they did have. The Supreme Court agreed with Houston and Marshall.

FIVE

Journey Southward

It was around this time that big changes were being made in the NAACP. The organization was originally put together by both African Americans and whites who sympathized with African Americans and wanted to see that they were treated fairly in society. But even in those early days, it was obvious that, sooner or later, African Americans would have to run the organization on their own. Plenty of white people would continue helping the organization through the years, and still do to this day. But at the highest levels, African Americans had to start calling the shots.

MARSHALL AND FRIENDS MOVE ON

One of the lawyers leading the legal fight for the NAACP was a white man named Nathan Margold. He had given years of hard work to the organization but had resigned in 1933 in the hopes that an African American would replace him. The NAACP took its time finding the right man, but when it did, it picked a great one—Charles Hamilton Houston. Houston left his teaching position at Howard University and moved to New York, specifically to the neighborhood of Harlem, where the NAACP had its main office. He had done great things at Howard University, but now he was ready to give the NAACP his full attention.

Houston had lofty ideas about what the organization should do in the years ahead. More and more people were giving their time and their talent to the organization, and others were giving generous sums of money. The NAACP was getting stronger all the time, and Houston knew

Harlem was known to some as "the capital of Black America." Nearly half a million African Americans lived there when the Marshalls moved in.

it could do some incredible things with its increased power. He hadn't been running the organization for long before he asked one of his favorite former students, Thurgood Marshall, to come and work by his side.

Marshall was thrilled. He and his wife left Baltimore and joined Houston in 1936. Having lived in the Baltimore area more or less his whole life, he wasn't sure what to expect in New York City. Surely, he thought, Harlem was a different world. It turned out to be just that, but in a wonderful and amazing way. It was not only the home of the NAACP but also the place where most of the important African Americans in the United States lived at that time. Artists, writers, and musicians were living and working together there. During his few free moments, Marshall and his wife would go to restaurants, cafes, museums, and nightclubs.

While the cultural aspect of Marshall's life certainly changed, the work aspect didn't—it was as demanding as ever. He and Houston

The Harlem Renaissance

After World War I ended in 1918, many African Americans in the United States moved to the northeastern states to find work. Many settled in the New York City neighborhood of Harlem. Soon, Harlem was home to some of the best African American poets, writers, actors, painters, and musicians of the time, such as Langston Hughes and Zora Neale Hurston. For the first time, their work was being taken seriously by the rest of the country. This era of great creativity was known as the Harlem Renaissance.

continued searching for cases they could win that would not only help their clients lead better lives but also lead to changes in the law that would help all African Americans. But there was a problem. Although the NAACP was certainly making a difference in New York, it was having little effect in other parts of the country. There were regions in the United States in which discrimination was still out of control, where African Americans had little chance of leading a decent life.

INTO THE LION'S DEN

The worst places for discrimination was the Deep South. The Deep South is a loose term that designated the southern parts of the country, specifically anywhere below something called the Mason-Dixon Line. This line is essentially the border that separates Pennsylvania from its neighbor to the south, Maryland. The line separated the states that did not permit slavery before the Civil War (all those north of the line) from those that did (all those south).

The Mason-Dixon Line

The Mason-Dixon Line got its name from the two British astronomers, Charles Mason and Jeremiah Dixon, who were asked to determine precisely where Pennsylvania ended and Maryland began. This grew out of a battle between the families who supposedly owned the two states—the Calverts (Maryland) and the Penns (Pennsylvania).

African Americans considered the northern states friendlier because a great deal of the hatred toward them that existed in the Deep South was kept alive even after slavery was abolished. Some families of former slave owners passed down to their children their negative attitudes toward African Americans, which included their belief that whites were superior people. Even though slavery was illegal, the thinking that allowed it to occur in the first place had not changed for many people. Some African Americans found it almost impossible to find jobs, buy homes, go shopping, or go to school. They were mistreated everywhere they went, sometimes while the police stood by doing nothing. Some believed that the farther south an African American went, the less friendly the people tended to become. Thus, the term "Deep South" held disturbing implications for the average African American citizen.

In spite of all this, Charles Hamilton Houston knew the NAACP would have to make some friends in the Deep South if African Americans were ever to enjoy true equality in the United States. So, even though he asked Marshall to join him in New York, it wasn't long before he asked his favorite former student to pack his bags and head south into the lion's den. Houston didn't lie about the risks. He told Marshall flat-out that it would be dangerous work and that there probably would be instances when his life would be in jeopardy. But Marshall was a brave fighter, determined to push ahead and make progress.

At that time, even though the NAACP was receiving more and more donations, it still wasn't exactly swimming in money. During his journeys to the South in the late 1930s, Marshall sometimes found himself sleeping in filthy hotels, paying for his own food, and conducting business in his car. But he felt all the hardships were worth it. He found hundreds of people, both African American and white, who were not only interested in helping the NAACP but also relieved to see that such an organization had finally found the courage to reach into the Deep South in the first place.

Marshall wasn't the only person living dangerously. Some of the white people who offered to help the NAACP would only do so in

Marshall, at far right, holds an antiracism poster in Mississippi. Marshall took many trips into the southern United States in an attempt to unite the African American communities and defeat racism. Angry whites would threaten his life, forcing him to sleep in different places each night and rely on the protection of friends bearing arms.

secret. They had to *live* in the Deep South, after all—Marshall was only visiting. If someone who hated African Americans found out his white neighbor was helping the NAACP, that neighbor might come home one night to find his house burned to the ground.

If Marshall was upset by the way African Americans were treated in the North, then what he saw in the Deep South must have chilled him. In the North, an African American teacher might not get paid the same salary as a white one. But in the southern states, an African American teacher, no matter how qualified or brilliant, might never be able to get a job at all. If an African American committed a crime in the north, he or she might be treated roughly by the police. In the Deep South, African Americans were sometimes beaten and thrown in jail without a trial, sometimes for doing nothing wrong. Even though African Americans were, technically, allowed to vote in the southern states, Marshall discovered that very few of them did. If they showed up at polling stations to vote on election day, the people who ran the voting booths would often throw them out. If they insisted on voting, they might get beaten up a few days later. Marshall realized that life was much worse for African Americans living in the Deep South. When word began to spread among southern African Americans about what Marshall was trying to do, they began thinking of him as something of a savior.

A NEW MAN TAKES CHARGE

In 1938, Charles Hamilton Houston left the NAACP for health reasons. He had been struggling with tuberculosis for some time, and now it was compounded by heart problems. On his way out of office, he picked

The Ku Klux Klan marches in Washington in 1925. The Klan was formed in Pulaski, Tennessee, immediately after the Civil War. The organizers were six former officers from the Confederate Army. The name "Ku Klux" comes from the Greek *kuklos*, which means "circle."

Marshall to be his replacement. At the age of thirty, Thurgood Marshall found himself making all the legal decisions for the largest and most successful African American organization in the country.

Even though he was the NAACP's chief counsel, Marshall continued his dangerous road trips rather than assign them to someone else. In Texas, a police chief threatened to attack him. When Marshall finally met the chief face-to-face, a Texas state trooper had to protect him.

Another time, Marshall was driving around in search of people to help him with an upcoming case and was followed by members of a group called the Ku Klux Klan. Also called the KKK, it was a secret organization of people who believed whites were the strongest and greatest race on Earth and that all other races were inferior. Its members held a particular hatred for African Americans and would often act against them with brutal violence. When Marshall was in areas where there were many KKK members, he often slept in a different place every night, traveled secretly in other people's cars, and had to be accompanied by armed guards.

Some days, Marshall's work was frightening and a little discouraging. Other days, however, were much better. As the NAACP's influence grew, so did the number of people who offered to help the organization. One of them was Donald Murray, the man Marshall helped gain admission into the law school at the University of Maryland. Murray was only too happy to tender his services to the lawyer who had helped him get his education, and make a little history at the same time.

The political climate in the United States was changing at the highest levels in favor of African Americans. But, at the same time, the

The Great Depression

In the 1920s, people were spending money faster than they could earn it. They bought items on credit, which means they didn't have to pay for them until later. Eventually, people bought too much on credit and could buy no more. That caused a depression, which is a time when there is little money in the economy and few jobs. Some people suddenly had no place to live, very little food, and only the clothes on their backs. This period lasted from 1929 until the early 1940s.

economic climate of the country was suffering. The country had fallen into its worst economic depression in 1929. Thousands of people lost their jobs and their money. Families were struggling just to eat. Clearly, it was time for some new leadership for the country.

SIX

A Time of Change

In 1932, the United States elected Franklin Delano Roosevelt as its president. Roosevelt, a Democrat, was familiar with the plight of African Americans and wanted to improve their situation. Unlike many past presidents, he invited leading African American figures to the White House and listened to what they had to say. This group became known as Roosevelt's "Black Cabinet." In presidential politics, a cabinet is a group of people the president feels he can trust for advice on important matters. The prominent African Americans in this group included A. Philip Randolph, the president of the Brotherhood of Sleeping Car Porters; Mary McLeod Bethune, director of Negro Affairs in the National Youth Administration (NYA); and Robert Weaver, who would later become the head of a government office called the Department of Housing and Urban Development.

One of the most effective changes instituted by Roosevelt—and one that Thurgood Marshall appreciated greatly—was altering the U.S. Supreme Court. The Supreme Court was the most powerful court in the country. Every decision it made had an effect on the future of the United States. It was composed of nine judges called justices, and, until Franklin D. Roosevelt became president, most were unlikely to agree to changes that would help African Americans.

Roosevelt changed that. During his four-term presidency, which lasted from 1933 until his death in 1945, he replaced many of these judges with new ones—those who were much more likely to hand down rulings in favor of African Americans. For Thurgood Marshall, who never stopped dreaming of eliminating segregation once and for all, this was very good news indeed.

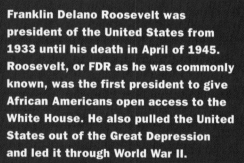

Franklin Delano Roosevelt was president of the United States from 1933 until his death in April of 1945. Roosevelt, or FDR as he was commonly known, was the first president to give African Americans open access to the White House. He also pulled the United States out of the Great Depression and led it through World War II.

SAYING GOOD-BYE TO OLD FRIENDS

Marshall suffered a tremendous loss in 1950. Charles Hamilton Houston died of a heart attack. In spite of having become one of the finest lawyers in the country, Marshall still turned to Houston for help and advice. Now, he would truly be on his own. However, in the weeks and months leading up to his death, Houston, from his hospital bed, worked with Marshall on their plan to end segregation. He did not want to leave Marshall without something to build on after he was gone.

By the time Houston died, so had President Roosevelt. The man who succeeded him was his vice president, Harry S. Truman. Like Roosevelt, Truman was a Democrat. He came from the state of Missouri, where discrimination was rampant. He had seen the way African

African Americans in World War II

When the United States entered World War II in 1941, many African American citizens bravely enlisted. For the first time in its 167-year history, the Marine Corps asked African Americans to join its ranks. This war also produced the first African American general, Brigadier General Benjamin O. Davis, Sr. Thousands of African Americans left their loved ones behind and traveled to Europe and Asia, defending a country that didn't always treat them well. These men fought in spite of this, many losing their lives in the process.

Americans were treated all his life, so when he became president, he decided to do something to change the situation.

Thousands of African Americans had fought bravely in World War II, which, for the United States, lasted from 1941 to 1945. Truman, like many others, believed that if African Americans were willing to fight and die for their country, they should be given as much respect as anyone else. Until his presidency, African Americans were not treated equally in the armed forces—discrimination was present even there.

In 1948, Truman issued an order that all discriminatory practices be banned not only in the military but also in all government jobs. Truman also put together a group of people, both white and African American, to conduct an in-depth study of the race problem in the United States. He wasn't just pretending he cared about the problem, like some political leaders did. Truman really wanted to make changes.

Marshall and the rest of the NAACP were happy to see that positive changes were occurring elsewhere around the country too. One of the most famous examples was in professional sports. Jackie Robinson became the first African American to play major league baseball. Until Robinson was given this opportunity, only whites were allowed to play in the major leagues. African American ballplayers had to play in what was known as the Negro Leagues. Jackie Robinson's acceptance into the major leagues was an enormous step for African Americans, and it showed in a very public way that attitudes toward African Americans were changing.

MARSHALL RENEWS HIS DETERMINATION

While Marshall and the NAACP were making tremendous progress, the issue of segregation in U.S. schools still bothered them. It was like a bad

Jackie Robinson's Difficult Early Years in Baseball

Many white players opposed the idea of integrating professional sports. Some tried to hurt Robinson during games. Pitchers would throw the ball at his head, while others would try to kick him with their cleats. This only strengthened Robinson's determination. He became one of the greatest players of his time, with a career that spanned from 1947 to 1956. He was elected to the National Baseball Hall of Fame in 1962.

cough that wouldn't go away. Marshall firmly believed the key to gaining equality for African Americans lay in the nation's educational system. This was logical and sensible—if African Americans couldn't be assured of a quality education, what chance did they have to succeed in society? They couldn't get ahead if they couldn't get good jobs, and they couldn't get good jobs if they didn't have a good education. So this barrier had to be broken down.

What Marshall was fighting was not only the idea of segregation, but also a legal decision made in the 1896 case *Plessy* v. *Ferguson*. This case set an ugly precedent that African Americans would have to struggle against for decades. The case involved a man named Homer Plessy. He was an African American living in Louisiana. After the Civil War, African Americans were supposedly permitted all the freedoms and opportunities the country had to offer through the Fourteenth Amendment to the Constitution. Many of the people living in the Deep South, however, where feelings against African Americans were strongest, decided to create communities where African Americans were treated anything but equally. They made sure African Americans were kept well apart from whites. African Americans were unable to eat in the same restaurants as whites, unable to shop in the same stores, live in the same towns, or go to the same schools. There were many other examples of segregation, including African Americans being denied the privilege of riding on the same trains as whites.

Homer Plessy had agreed to take part in a plan formed by a group called the Citizens' Committee to Test the Constitutionality of the Separate Car Law. This law, which was being enforced in Louisiana, stated that all railroads had to provide separate cars on their trains for African Americans so they wouldn't ride in the same cars as whites. The

Citizens' Committee felt this rule violated the U.S. Constitution, so they decided to put it to the test. In June of 1892, the committee sent Plessy onto one of the trains. He bought a first-class ticket and then sat in one of the cars meant for white people. Although of African heritage, Plessy was very light skinned and could easily pass as a white man. However, the people running the railroad were told that an African American was sitting in one of the "white cars"—this was part of the Committee's plan—and Plessy was arrested. He was brought to court and put before a judge named John Ferguson. Ferguson planned to fine Plessy for breaking the law. But before he had the chance, Plessy sued him, and the case was brought to the U.S. Supreme Court, which was exactly what the Citizens' Committee wanted.

Plessy's lawyers, who were white but had fought for the rights of many African Americans in the past, said the law that forbade Plessy from riding in the whites-only car was a violation of the Constitution's Fourteenth Amendment. The Supreme Court ruled against Plessy. The justices said the train cars designed for African Americans were just as good as the whites-only cars, so Plessy had no good reason not to use them. This decision became known as the separate-but-equal doctrine, and it gave people who felt African Americans to be inferior to whites tremendous strength. In the years to come, they argued that the Supreme Court had already decided that the separate-but-equal rule was constitutional. This rule was used to keep African Americans separate from whites in more places than just trains—it was applied pretty much everywhere.

Thurgood Marshall's goal, to overturn a decision made by the Supreme Court, was a lofty one. To overturn a decision means to reverse or undo it, and overturning a decision made by the highest court in the land is extremely rare. This is law in its most powerful form, fought by people who feel strongly about their beliefs. It was the kind of fight that leads to changes in the entire country, sometimes the world.

THE BEGINNING OF THE MOST IMPORTANT CASE OF ALL

The battle began in 1950 in Clarendon County, South Carolina. There, a couple named Harry and Liza Briggs filed a lawsuit against the state because they felt one of their children was being forced to go to an elementary school whose facilities were not equal to those of the elementary school for whites. In Clarendon, as in many other places in the South, segregation was common practice—*that* part of the separate-but-equal rule was being followed to the letter. But the equal part was being ignored.

Not long after the Briggses filed their lawsuit, they began getting harassed by people who lived nearby and hated African Americans. Maybe this wasn't every white person in the area, but it was enough of them to make the situation frightening. The Briggses were told to give up their lawsuit and to leave things the way they were. They knew that some African Americans who had been bold enough to fight racial discrimination in the past had been physically beaten; some were even killed. This didn't happen to them, but they still endured certain "punishments." At one point, for example, they were both fired from their jobs. They felt they were fighting an important battle, however, so they bravely fought on.

Marshall heard about this situation and decided to help. He reviewed the facts of the case and realized it would be an easy victory— there were considerably more African Americans in the Clarendon area

This is a segregated school in Georgia, circa 1941. Many African American schools had low-grade housing, outdated books, and minimal funding—even though state governments had promised money for improvement.

than there were whites, yet the bulk of the money set aside for education went to the white schools. Also, the teachers working in the white schools were being paid much higher salaries than the teachers working in the African American schools.

Marshall also thought this case would be an ideal opportunity to attack segregation overall. At first, he hid the attack within the case, but the judge, who was sympathetic to Marshall's cause, told him to change his approach and to make his attack on segregation the main argument. Marshall was afraid he might lose on that basis. Losing the case would mean he could then bring it to the U.S. Supreme Court, which was a good thing. But losing also meant he couldn't help the Briggses immediately, which distressed him. In the end, he decided to follow the judge's advice and focus on the broader issue.

Meanwhile, South Carolina's governor, James Byrnes, heard about the case and decided the last thing he wanted was to have the case go to the Supreme

Court. He had been justice on the Supreme Court from 1941 to 1942. If the case went to the Supreme Court, he knew there was a chance Marshall would able to end school segregation across the entire nation. That would mean an end to segregation in South Carolina, which Byrnes did not want.

Byrnes's solution to this problem was to immediately put great sums of money toward the improvement of African American schools throughout South Carolina. The teachers would get equal pay, the classrooms would have the same books and other supplies, and leaky roofs would be fixed. He was only too happy to meet these demands, claiming he was doing it because it was the right and decent thing to do.

When the Briggs case went to court in May of 1951, the lawyers who represented the state of South Carolina admitted that the schools for African Americans were far from equal to those for whites. They didn't want to argue the point because facts spoke for themselves. By doing this, they wanted to end the case quickly, give Marshall his victory, and get out of court quickly.

Marshall knew what they were up to and wasn't going to fall for it. He changed the whole focus of the case by arguing that South Carolina should give up its discriminatory practices and outlaw segregation entirely. He presented data that suggested segregation was harmful to young African Americans, that it made them feel that they were worth less than whites were. He argued that it was impossible to create environments that were truly separate but equal because, in the words of his dear friend Charles Hamilton Houston, "There is no such thing as separate-but-equal. Segregation itself imports inequality."

Marshall lost the case on that basis, which was what the state's lawyers wanted to avoid. The court said that the only violation that was committed was not ensuring that the schools for African Americans were equal to those for whites. That wasn't enough of a cause for the court to outlaw segregation entirely. The court ordered that the state immediately begin bringing schools for African Americans up to the standards of the schools for whites.

Marshall pored over thousands of pages of legal text to find a way to get the issue of school segregation to the Supreme Court. He knew it would be a constitutional issue, and he was confident he could have it abolished.

Marshall presented the case to the U.S. Supreme Court. He was ready to use the same argument—school segregation was wrong, even if the schools for African Americans were just as good as those for whites. He was deeply saddened when the Supreme Court refused to hear the case. In January of 1952, the court sent the case back to the South Carolina court to find out how much better the segregated schools had become. The state court decided that the Briggs case was handled properly and that nothing had been done wrong. Marshall was very upset.

Marshall's next plan was to bring the case back to the Supreme Court yet again. This time, however, he brought a few other people along with him—people involved in similar lawsuits around the country. He decided that he had made a mistake by bringing only the Briggs case to the Supreme Court. He was asking the Supreme Court to undo what South Carolina had done, which really wasn't what he wanted at all. What he wanted was to bring up the issue of whether school segregation should be allowed anywhere in the United States.

SEVEN

Making History

Marshall's new case became known as *Brown* v. *Board of Education*, so named because of a case in Kansas involving a local board of education and a family whose last name was Brown. Amazingly, in that case, a group of judges had ruled that school segregation had a negative impact on African American children. School segregation made them believe less in themselves and that there was something wrong with them because they weren't good enough to go to school with white children. The fact that the laws in Kansas and elsewhere around the country upheld this belief only made the African American children feel worse. As a result, the children did not try as hard in school, for they did not believe they would ever amount to much, no matter how hard they worked.

The lawyer who was hired to fight against Thurgood Marshall was a man named John W. Davis. Davis was known as one of the best lawyers in the country. Ironically, even though Davis and Marshall would be arguing against each other, Marshall admired Davis greatly. He even once said, "I learned most of my stuff from him." He thought Davis was one of the most brilliant lawyers he'd ever seen. He even admitted to thinking he could never be as good as Davis when it came to courtroom arguments.

Nevertheless, Marshall had a job to do, so he set aside any feelings of intimidation he may have had. He looked further into the segregation-hurts-the-children approach, gathering psychological studies that supported his case. He was disturbed by what he learned through this research. African American children had even less self-esteem that he imagined. Even though some of them were treated poorly by whites in society, many of them still believed whites were the better race and they, purely because of the color of their skin, were worse.

Marshall chats with John W. Davis, his opponent in the *Brown* v. *Board of Education* case. Although they were legal rivals, Marshall openly admired Davis's legendary skills in a courtroom. During his long and distinguished career, Davis was also an ambassador, solicitor general, and presidential candidate.

Marshall knew this was nonsense and intended to prove it. He worked day and night getting ready for the case, denying himself food and sleep, sometimes going for days at a time without rest. He pushed the people who were helping him just as hard. Soon the entire country heard about this important case and began to take notice.

SUPREME COURT, SUPREME BATTLEFIELD

The case formally began on December 9, 1952. There were crowds on the steps of the Supreme Court building, including reporters and photographers. Inside, Marshall and his team were invited to speak first. Not long after they began, some tough questions were thrown at them. The Court was curious about whether it was being asked to eliminate school segregation simply because some people felt it was wrong. Segregation had been the law for a long time, and many other

The Varied History of John W. Davis

John William Davis was born in 1873 in Clarksburg, West Virginia. His academic brilliance was obvious from an early age. He graduated from Washington and Lee College in 1895 and became a teacher there the following year. He opened his own law firm shortly thereafter and soon became involved in politics. He ran for the presidency of the United States in 1924, as a Democrat, but was defeated by Republican Calvin Coolidge.

cases had been based on it. The justices wondered why they should consider changing it now.

Marshall turned this argument around and said the justices should outlaw segregation because it was morally wrong and hurt children without good reason. He reasoned that segregation ". . . deprived them of equal status in the school community." The fact that the country had been practicing segregation for such a long time didn't automatically make it right.

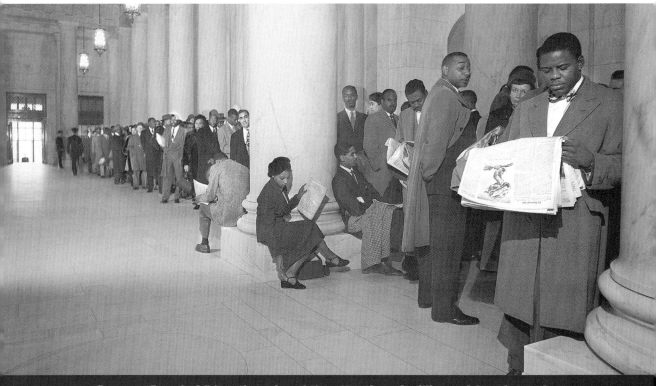

Brown v. *Board of Education* **gripped the attention of millions of Americans. In this photo from December of 1952, hundreds eagerly await news of the latest developments in Washington, D.C.**

Another tough question was asked. What could he say about the reality that discrimination existed whether or not schoolchildren were segregated? What could he say about the safety of African American children if they started attending previously all-white schools? Simply forcing African American and white children to learn together wasn't going to wipe out the bad feelings some whites had toward African Americans.

Marshall argued that these excuses for upholding segregation were not good enough. They gave people who hated African Americans too much power. They had to be fought. He also believed that many people in the country had become smarter about the race issue and would be more in favor of ending segregation. More people, he believed, agreed with him than ever before.

Marshall also discussed his psychological findings, providing a great deal of information from some of the most respected psychologists in the world. It was clear that segregation was doing African American children great harm. By reducing their belief in themselves, it also reduced how far they could hope to go in life. This, Marshall said, proved that a true separate-but-equal situation was impossible to achieve. By keeping the children separate, they would never feel equal. This evidence was impossible to ignore. The nine justices on the Supreme Court had to do something about it.

When Marshall was finished arguing his side of the case, John Davis got his turn. Using a deep, penetrating voice that echoed through the courtroom and demanded complete attention, he argued that segregation should in fact not be eliminated. The heart of his argument was the same one Marshall had heard a million times. Segregation had always been the law, so it should stay the law. One of the Supreme Court justices asked Davis why he felt the law could not be changed. Wasn't it sometimes the very job of the Supreme Court to update the laws of the country in order to keep up with changing times? Davis said it was but

The 1952 Supreme Court heard the first part of the case and then sent both sides away with some questions to consider about the Constitution's Fourteenth Amendment. Chief Justice Frederick Moore Vinson (seated front row, center) favored leaving segregation alone, but he would die of a heart attack before the Court reconvened in May of 1954 to hand down its final ruling.

not in this case. The people who originally decided on segregation did not mean for it to be changed. It was their intention, he said, to keep African American schoolchildren apart from white schoolchildren.

The point that Davis seemed to be missing, which was also the whole point of Marshall's side of the argument, was that separating African American schoolchildren from white schoolchildren had no value. Why was it being done? Marshall had a feeling he knew why so many people wanted it kept that way—because many whites felt that African Americans were, in fact, lower and lesser than whites.

Davis would never, ever admit this in front of the Supreme Court. But Marshall felt he had found the weak spot he was looking for. What the whole case came down to was what the Supreme Court believed. Maybe the Supreme Court justices back in 1896 really did think African Americans were unequal to whites. But did the justices believe it now? As part of his closing remarks, he said, "There is nothing involved in this case other than race and color." That, he knew, was the point on which the entire case would turn.

QUESTIONS TO PONDER

On June 8, 1953, the Supreme Court made a decision. It wasn't a final decision as Marshall had hoped, but it didn't shut down his case, either. The court said the case would be set aside for the time being so that both sides could spend some time thinking about the true meaning of the Constitution's Fourteenth Amendment. What was the intention of the people who created it? Was segregation meant only to be enforced during that particular time, or was it meant to be enforced forever? And was it really within the court's power to change that? Perhaps that was the most important question of all.

In the months that followed, Marshall's team and John Davis's team weren't the only ones who considered these questions. The president of the United States called a small group of government lawyers together to look into the matter. This group discovered some interesting facts. One was that the segregation laws were created not long after African Americans were freed from slavery and that African Americans had been given little education while they were slaves. At that time, the average African American child was far behind the average white child in schooling. Also, children were not required to go to school in those days, so many African American youngsters who came from poor families never saw the inside of a classroom. So perhaps segregation in schools was a good idea at that time because the average African American child needed a different type of schooling.

The Supreme Court justices also did a bit of their own research. After a long period of thorough and exhaustive research, they concluded that the people who originally designed a segregated school system made no mention of the idea that schools should stay segregated forever. This was not their intention, so perhaps there was, in fact, room for change.

Regardless of this research, it seemed as if the decision would be determined by what the nine Supreme Court justices felt was best for the country. There was no clear course, just the opinion of those nine men. John Davis was still confident they would deliver Marshall a defeat. Davis didn't need all nine to do this—he just needed the majority, or five justices. Marshall wasn't sure what would happen. The Supreme Court had become more liberal and open-minded in recent years, and that certainly was good for him and for all African Americans. But had it become open-minded enough? It was hard to say.

Then something quite unexpected happened. In September of 1953, Fred Vinson, the chief justice of the Supreme Court, suffered a heart attack and died. Vinson was one of the justices John Davis felt he could depend on to see things his way. He thought Vinson would help him win the case. Vinson's replacement was much more interested in helping African Americans than Vinson ever was. His name was Earl Warren.

With Warren as the new chief justice, Marshall felt better about the future of the case. He and the others returned to the Supreme Court on December 3, 1953, almost one year after they began the first half of it—ready to make history.

Again, Marshall was asked to speak first. He began by saying that he was

Earl Warren took over as Chief Justice of the Supreme Court after Frederick Vinson died. He was appointed by then-president Dwight D. Eisenhower and made considerable changes to laws concerning civil rights and the rights of the accused. He served until 1969 and died in July of 1974.

certain, after all his research, that the Fourteenth Amendment to the Constitution was designed to protect all citizens of the United States, including African Americans. There was absolutely no reason to treat African Americans as if they were inferior to whites. If the court truly wanted segregation to continue, he said, it would have to prove that African Americans were inferior to whites. He argued that those who wanted to keep school segregation in place were determined to make sure African Americans never improved themselves. And that, Marshall said, was not what the Fourteenth Amendment was all about. In fact, it was exactly the opposite of what the Fourteenth Amendment stated, and therefore segregation had to be eliminated.

John Davis again argued that the justices should stick with the existing law rather than change it. He insisted that schools equal to those reserved for whites would be built for African Americans. He said forcing

A Man of Integrity and Fairness

Earl Warren was born in California in 1891. He became California's governor in 1942 and was popular with members of both the Democratic and Republican parties. He considered himself a liberal Republican. He believed in smaller government and lower taxes, but he also believed in civil rights and equality for all people. He would serve as chief justice of the Supreme Court from 1953 until he retired in 1969. He died five years later.

African American schoolchildren and white schoolchildren together would cause trouble. People would fight the integration, and some people would get hurt. He asked the justices if they really thought it was a good idea to dispose of segregation based on ". . . some fancied question of racial prestige." He wanted to convince the Supreme Court that it was, in fact, good for African American schoolchildren to be segregated for their own safety.

THE DAM BURSTS AT LAST

When Thurgood Marshall and John Davis were finished offering their arguments, the nine justices set aside a few months to discuss and consider the issue. Chief Justice Warren already knew how he felt. He agreed with Marshall that segregation had to go. And he knew some of the other judges felt the same way. But he also felt it was important that all nine justices eventually agree on a decision. If it were only five or six in favor of changing the law, many people would feel the Supreme Court hadn't been fully behind the decision. He wanted the people of the United States to know that the Supreme Court was acting as one unified force. He wanted the matter closed once and for all.

On May 17, 1954, Chief Justice Warren made the announcement. Speaking for all nine justices, he declared that educational segregation no longer had a place in U.S. society, that it denied African American schoolchildren valuable and necessary opportunities, and that it hurt them in ways that would affect them throughout their lives. "Segregation of white and colored children in public schools has a detrimental effect upon the colored children," he wrote in the formal decision. He said it

may have had a value and a purpose at an earlier time, but that time had passed. "Whatever may have been the extent of psychological knowledge at the time of *Plessy* v. *Ferguson*, this finding is amply supported by modern authority," Warren continued. "Any language in *Plessy* v. *Ferguson* contrary to this finding is rejected." Then Warren wrote, "We conclude that, in the field of public education, the doctrine of separate but equal has no place."

The Supreme Court ruled that school segregation in the United States be abolished forever.

There were smiles all around—Marshall, (center) along with George E. C. Hayes (left) and James M. Nabrit (right) on May 17, 1954, the day the Supreme Court abolished school segregation in the United States. Losing attorney John W. Davis would die less than a year after the decision. Some friends said the devastating loss of this case contributed to his death.

EIGHT

The Fight Goes On

Thurgood Marshall was probably the happiest man in the world in the days that followed the Supreme Court decision. All those years of hard work had finally paid off. Marshall became a celebrity, giving interviews on radio and television. He said that, at long last, African American people now had the means to wipe out segregation not only in the U.S. public school system but also in every other part of society, as well. In time, he was sure, there would be no more whites-only bathrooms, whites-only department stores, and whites-only restaurants. Eventually, African Americans would be able to enjoy all the same freedoms, privileges, and luxuries as everyone else. He was quoted in a speech as saying that the judgment of every citizen should be based on ". . . individual merit" rather than ". . . such irrelevant considerations as race and color."

Marshall and his second wife, Cissy, in September of 1958, stand outside the Supreme Court Building. On this day the Court ordered the school board of Little Rock, Arkansas to begin permitting African American students in their schools. The board of Little Rock was just one of many trying to resist desegregation until the last possible moment.

Sadly, however, this happy time didn't last long. Marshall's wife of more than twenty years, Vivian, told him she was dying of cancer. She had known about her illness for a while, but had kept it from him so he wouldn't be distracted from his work. As soon as he found out, he reduced his workload and spent as much time with her as possible. He cooked and cleaned for her and prayed that she would make a miraculous recovery. She never did. She died on February 11, 1955. Marshall felt as if his world had fallen apart. He and Vivian had been together for so long that they were like one soul in two bodies.

Marshall was not alone for long. He got married again about a year later to a woman named Cecilia Suyat. She was also known as "Cissy." Marshall met her while she was working as a secretary at the NAACP office in Harlem. While he and Vivian never had any children, he and Cissy would have two, Thurgood Jr., and John.

MASSIVE RESISTANCE

Now that his personal life was back in order and school segregation had been outlawed, Marshall turned his energies toward another challenge—making sure all U.S. schools honored the new antisegregation law. He knew the full desegregation of every school in the country would take time, but he also knew there were schools run by people who didn't want it to happen at all. These people would fight integration as long as they could and would have to be forced to do it. This attitude was strong, particularly in the Deep South, and became known as "massive resistance." Marshall said of this, "The other side planned all the delaying tactics they could think of."

The massive-resistance movement led to some horrible events. Bricks were thrown through the windows of African Americans' homes with notes attached that warned the families not to send their children to all-white schools. Children were spit on and beaten. Parents lost their jobs or couldn't get loans at local banks. If an African American owned a store, many white customers wouldn't shop there anymore. Worst of all, some schools still refused to let African American students enroll. They would rather risk getting in trouble with the federal government. There were days when even the local police refused to help with the situation. At one point, President Eisenhower had to call in the National Guard, a branch of the U.S. military, to protect a group of African American children who were trying to enter their new school in Little Rock, Arkansas.

Marshall was enraged by this. In some states, the governors tried to get around the new laws by pretending to be deeply concerned about the welfare and safety of the African American students, saying it was in their best interests not to be in the same schools with white children. But Marshall knew they were just trying to keep the schools segregated.

Once again, he turned to the Supreme Court for help, and once again it came through for him. In September of 1958, all nine justices agreed that changes in the law handed down by the Supreme Court could not be ignored on the state level. That meant state governors did

Even when African American students were finally permitted to attend Little Rock schools, they were met with anger and hatred. Eventually, the National Guard had to be called in to protect them—and fend off would be attackers.

not have the power to ignore a new law simply because they didn't like it. The justices made it clear that they weren't going to allow the law to be ignored under the threat of violence. Marshall was very pleased to get such strong backing for his position. In the long run, he knew segregation would be wiped out.

MARSHALL MOVES WITH THE TIMES

The exciting chapter in Marshall's life that involved heroically marching into the nation's highest courtroom and fighting for historic changes to the law was, for the most part, coming to a close. The Civil Rights Movement in the United States was evolving, driven largely by a new generation of activists.

Many of these younger people, while grateful to Marshall and the NAACP for everything they had done to further the African American cause, were also more impatient than Marshall, unwilling to spend months and years in slow-moving legal battles. This younger generation wanted to take the fight for equal rights out of the courts and into the streets. While Marshall was just as anxious to make changes that would help African Americans, he wanted to do it legally. Many of the younger activists, on the other hand, felt that stepping outside the law would produce results more quickly.

One of these activists was Dr. Martin Luther King, Jr. King was still in his twenties when he began gaining fame and influence in the United States. The son of a minister, he was a dazzling speaker, able to hold large crowds spellbound with his fiery and impassioned speeches. While he preached his strong belief in love and nonviolence, he was also willing to

The Life of Dr. Martin Luther King, Jr.

King was born in Georgia in 1929. He gained fame when he encouraged people in Alabama not to ride buses after an African American woman was ordered to give up her seat on a bus to a white man. In 1957, he formed the SCLC (Southern Christian Leadership Conference), an organization devoted to fighting segregation in the southern states. He was murdered in 1968 in Memphis, Tennessee. The United States celebrates his birthday as a national holiday on the third Monday in January.

break a law or two occasionally in order to get his point across. If, for example, there was a restaurant that did not permit African Americans to sit at its lunch counter, he would encourage local African Americans to sit there anyway.

While King and Marshall certainly had the same goal—to assure that African Americans would achieve equality—they did not agree on how to reach it. They weren't enemies, but it would be a stretch of the truth to say they were friends. King appreciated what the NAACP had done for African Americans, but he felt the organization could do more. One thing he wanted it to do, from time to time, was pay legal bills for him and his colleagues whenever they got into trouble. If King and some of his followers walked through the streets of a town carrying anti-segregation signs and were arrested for disturbing the peace, he might ask Marshall and others at the NAACP for the money he needed to get everyone out of jail.

NEW ALLIES

Realizing that times were changing and that he had to change with them, Marshall kept his eyes and ears open for new opportunities to fight for equality. In 1960, the United States elected a new president, John F. Kennedy. Kennedy was unlike any other president before him—young, handsome, and full of new ideas and visions that matched the country's youth. A northern Democrat, he was probably one of the most liberal presidents the country has ever had. He was strongly supported by African Americans during his campaign and owed them a huge debt. As a believer in equality and civil rights, he planned to repay that debt in full.

He appointed his brother, Robert Kennedy, to be the nation's attorney general. The attorney general is the head lawyer for the U.S. government. He or she advises the president and other high-ranking members of the government on important legal matters. The attorney general also represents the government in important cases. It is a tremendously important job.

Robert Kennedy knew Thurgood Marshall, and he felt there could be a place for Marshall in his older brother's new government. Marshall had an idea about that, too—he wanted to become a judge on the Court of Appeals. Generally speaking, the Court of Appeals decides which cases will be heard by the Supreme Court.

There was a position open on the Court of Appeals when Marshall first talked with Robert Kennedy. Kennedy, however, said he already had

Marshall (center) talks with Republican senator Jacob Javits (left) and Democratic senator Robert Kennedy (right). After Marshall was designated the next U.S. Solicitor General by President Lyndon Johnson, Kennedy said, "He will make one of the great solicitor generals in the history of this country."

someone else in mind for the position, so he offered Marshall a different one. It was a lower position—about one step below the Court of Appeals—and Marshall flatly told Kennedy he didn't want it. He said he wanted the Court of Appeals job or none at all.

Over time, Robert Kennedy decided that Marshall really was the best choice for the Court of Appeals position, and he said so to his brother. African Americans needed people from their own race to occupy positions of influence and power. The president had promised he would help make this happen and appointed Marshall to the Court of Appeals. There were many people in the government, especially those who represented the Deep South, who didn't want Marshall to have the job. They fought unsuccessfully to keep him from getting the appointment.

Going from being a lawyer to being judge was a big step for Marshall, and in many ways he was unprepared. Although he was an expert in civil rights and on the struggle of African Americans, he was not an expert in other areas. As an appeals court judge, he needed to be. He had to learn, sometimes on the fly, about everything from taxation to international law. It was all new territory for him, but he did what he had to do to get by. Soon, he was being praised by people who previously had wondered if he could handle the position.

A DAY THAT CHANGED THE WORLD

Just when it seemed as if the political climate in the United States was changing in favor of African American causes, tragedy struck. On November 22, 1963, President Kennedy was assassinated in Dallas, Texas, while riding in a convertible with the top down.

The Kennedy presidency came to an abrupt end, and with it went the hopes of many African Americans for a brighter future. They regarded Kennedy as dependable ally, someone who, in his brief presidential tenure, had already fought for them many times and would have done so again.

Thurgood Marshall, Father and Husband

Although Marshall was, by nature, an incredibly busy and active man, he always found time for his wife, Cissy, and their two boys, Thurgood, Jr.—who was nicknamed "Goody"—and John. When the boys were young, Marshall would play with them. They would play simple card games or run an electric train set. Marshall also liked to cook for his family and sometimes for groups of friends. Marshall rarely disciplined his children, leaving that responsibility to his wife. He once said that he couldn't bring himself to punish the boys for anything he'd done wrong himself as a child.

NINE

Another Moment in History

The man who replaced Kennedy was his vice president, Lyndon Baines Johnson, who was commonly known by his initials, LBJ. Johnson was a tall, lanky Texan who shared Kennedy's interest in civil rights. He, too, was familiar with the many achievements of Thurgood Marshall and admired him very much.

Johnson was interested in keeping many of Kennedy's projects and ideas alive. One important example was his signing of the Civil Rights Act of 1964. This was, without question, the most powerful package of civil rights laws in the history of the nation. It outlawed discrimination in the workplace, in public places such as restaurants and hotels, and in voting booths during elections. It also promised that any people or

A great moment in history for African Americans was the day President Lyndon Johnson signed the 1964 Civil Rights Act into law. Legislators in the Deep South fought it with all their might, and Johnson earned thousands of enemies as a result. Marshall once said of Johnson, "I loved that man."

institutions receiving money from the federal government would lose that money if they were caught practicing discrimination in any form.

A HUGE STEP IN THE RIGHT DIRECTION

Johnson knew the Civil Rights Act of 1964 would meet with a great deal of resistance. A lot of people would try to ignore the new laws. He needed to find the right person to make sure that didn't happen. In July of 1965, he offered Marshall the position of solicitor general. "Well, Mr. President, I'll have to think it over," Marshall replied during their phone call. The next day, he had made his decision. He would become the first African American solicitor general in the nation's history.

The job of the solicitor general is to argue cases before the Supreme Court on behalf of the government. It is not as secure a position as the position of appeals court judge even the pay is less. For Marshall, however, it would be a step up in many ways. The solicitor general is one of the most powerful lawyers in the nation, and Marshall would be the first African American ever to hold the job. He would also have access to the president at all times—in that capacity he certainly could do wonderful things for the people of his race. Because Johnson liked Marshall and listened to him, Marshall knew he could accomplish a great deal in the new position.

Lyndon Johnson was often a confusing figure to the African American people. On the one hand, he stood before millions and promised he would fight for the rights of those who had been denied equality in the past. He signed the Civil Rights Act of 1964 and gave Marshall opportunities that had never before been given to an African American.

On the other hand, he could also be brash and crude, often using profane language openly and freely. Like many other African Americans, Marshall must have decided that a person's actions were more important than his or her words. Regardless of whatever hurtful words rolled out of his mouth, Johnson was doing more for African Americans than any other president had done since Abraham Lincoln abolished slavery in 1863. He didn't just promise to surround himself with a mixed-race staff, he actually did it. He chose, for example, an African American man named Robert Weaver to be a member of his cabinet. This was a first in the country's history.

Marshall began his new job as solicitor general on August 11, 1965. Just like a new president, a new solicitor general must place his hand on the Bible and recite an oath of office. By doing so, the person promises to do everything in his or her power to perform faithfully his or her new responsibilities. The person who holds the Bible and officially performs the ceremony is a Supreme Court justice. In Marshall's case, the justice was Hugo Black, a former Ku Klux Klan member who had had a change of heart earlier and decided to support African Americans rather than hate them. Marshall must have noticed the irony and symbolism of the moment. After he recited the oath, Justice Black commented publicly that he thought Marshall would do an excellent job.

One of Marshall's first major cases as solicitor general came the following November. It involved the murder of three young boys, two of whom were white, who had been traveling through Mississippi in June of 1964. They were trying to encourage African Americans to vote in upcoming elections. Their car was stopped on a quiet back road during the night, they were dragged into the open and shot at close range, and

Abraham Lincoln Frees Millions of Slaves

On January 1, 1863, then-president Abraham Lincoln issued his Emancipation Proclamation, which declared that all people who were being held as slaves in the Confederate states were free. At the time, the country was in the midst of a heated conflict known as the Civil War. It was a battle between the Union states in the North and the Confederate states in the South. The Emancipation Proclamation gave more than three million people their freedom. Two years later, the Thirteenth Amendment to the Constitution would abolish slavery everywhere in the country.

Marshall is sworn in as U.S. solicitor general. When asked if he could rule fairly on civil rights cases, Marshall replied, "I am an advocate and I represent the U.S.

their bodies were dumped into a ditch and then buried. A number of suspects were brought before the Mississippi courts, but no one was ever convicted of the crime. As it turned out, many people were involved— some in the actual killings, some in the ensuing cover-up. Marshall fought to have them brought to justice, and in the end seven people were sent to jail.

Another important case of Marshall's involved voting rights for African Americans. Like school segregation, Marshall considered voting rights a crucial piece of the equality puzzle. If African Americans were kept from voting for the leaders they supported, what chance did they have of having their views and beliefs reflected in the government?

To help in this endeavor, President Johnson created the Voting Rights Act of 1965. It stated clearly that all U.S. citizens, regardless of race, had the undeniable right to vote in any election. In the past, some states tried to keep African Americans and other minorities from voting by charging something called a poll tax, which was a fee that many African Americans couldn't afford, or by requiring them to pass certain tests, knowing many African Americans wouldn't be able to do so. The Voting Rights Act of 1965 abolished those practices.

Some of the people who held elections in Virginia decided to ignore the new laws and continue charging a poll tax. In response, a group of African Americans got together in 1966 to challenge them. A court in Virginia shot the case down, saying, in so many words, that the state had the right to run its elections however it pleased. Marshall heard of this decision and decided the Virginia court was wrong. He brought the case before the Supreme Court, and the nine justices agreed with Marshall. Virginia had to abolish the poll tax.

AN INTERESTING IDEA

Marshall brought a number of important cases before the Supreme Court and won almost all of them as solicitor general. His ever-growing experience, his natural legal instincts, and his tireless drive had turned him into one of the most brilliant lawyers in the world. He was even good enough, many thought, to be an actual member of the Supreme Court. But some wondered if that was possible for an African American.

Lyndon Johnson thought it was. Johnson knew there would be an opening on the Supreme Court because Justice Tom Clark was going to resign in early 1967. Presidents who had the chance to appoint a justice

The Voting Rights Act of 1965 put a stop to unfair methods of keeping African Americans from electing their preferred civil officials. Here, Marshall (right), along with Assistant Attorney General John Doar (left) and Attorney General Nicholas Katzenbach (center), arrives at the Supreme Court Building to fight attorneys from six southern states trying to stave off the Act.

Marshall performed admirably as U.S. solicitor general, treating his aides and other assistants as equals and always keeping an open mind to their thoughts and opinions. He easygoing nature and natural grasp of American law put him on the top of President Johnson's list of replacements when a seat on the Supreme Court became open in 1967.

President Johnson liked Marshall not only as a professional, but also as a person. They would often sit together in the White House, drinking and chatting like old friends. Here, Marshall calls his wife to deliver the news that Johnson has asked him to be the next associate justice of the Supreme Court.

to the Supreme Court also had the chance to make a clear statement about their feelings toward the country. The person they chose would help support their programs and ideas through his or her power on the court.

There were a few people Johnson had in mind for the position. One was a woman, a judge from California. That, too, would have been a first in U.S. history—there had never been a female justice on the Supreme Court. Johnson also considered a handful of other minority candidates.

In the end, Johnson decided that Thurgood Marshall was the right person for the job. He invited Marshall to the White House to discuss it. Realizing he was being given the chance to live the dream of every lawyer, Marshall accepted the offer.

A Time of Uncertainty

In the late 1960s, the United States was involved in a bloody war in Vietnam. Vietnam was formerly governed by the nation of France. Then, in 1946, some Vietnamese tried to break away from France and gain the country's independence. Others, however, were content to leave things as they were. This led Vietnam to split into two nations, North Vietnam and South Vietnam. North Vietnam became a communist country, which meant the government basically controlled everything. North Vietnam's leaders planned to take over South Vietnam, but the U.S. government didn't want this to happen so they sent U.S. soldiers to fight alongside South Vietnamese troops. Unfortunately, this did not go well. More than 50,000 U.S. soldiers were killed in the fighting. Back in the United States, many people marched through the streets to protest the war, carrying signs and clashing with police.

On June 13, 1967, President Johnson makes history. He announces that he has nominated Marshall to the Supreme Court, making Marshall the first African American to reach that high office. Martin Luther King, Jr., called the nomination "a momentous step towards a color-blind society."

TEN

A Bad Situation
Gets Worse

The initial thrill of the moment was not to last long, however. In spite of Johnson's hard work supporting civil rights, the United States had found its way into one of its darkest periods. At home, rioting in the nation's major cities was increasing. People were being hurt and sometimes killed, property was being destroyed, and hatred and anger were out of control.

Much of it was driven by racial tension. Johnson had promised a war on poverty, hoping to create what he called "The Great Society" in which everyone was treated equally and didn't want for food, clothing, or shelter. Even if a person weren't rich, Johnson promised, he or she would have the basic necessities to survive, plus opportunities that weren't previously available.

Unfortunately, his grand vision was never fulfilled. Many of the people who lived in the nation's inner cities found that they were still stuck in the same appalling conditions as before; in short, nothing had changed. Some people blamed Johnson. He had made many promises but hadn't come through on them. Because the majority of people living in these impoverished areas were minorities, many of them African American, they tended to blame whites in general for Johnson's failure.

Some of the African American leaders who believed that breaking the law was the best way for minorities to be granted equal rights went into these areas to encourage people to riot. Many of them were against Thurgood Marshall's slower methods of going to court and fighting laws directly. They knew the people who were suffering in the inner cities were angry, and they used that anger to incite destructive acts.

Marshall was disgusted by the violence. Although he had just as much fight in his heart as anyone else, he had always believed the way for the African American people to get ahead was by challenging and changing the law, not by breaking it. Regardless of his levelheaded and sensible approach, however, he had a tough time getting the Supreme Court position. In the United States, a president can recommend someone for a spot on the Supreme Court, but he or she can't simply hire the person. Instead, that person has to be approved by the U.S. Senate.

Some of the senators who had to review Johnson's appointment of Marshall thought having an African American on the Supreme Court while there were numerous race riots flaring up in the nation's cities was a bad idea. They really couldn't come out and say this, so they grilled

Marshall for days, instead, firing questions at him as if he had committed some kind of heinous crime. They argued that putting an African American in such a powerful position would only increase the tension

Marshall waits with his wife before taking the stand at the Senate hearing to confirm (or deny) his appointment to the Supreme Court. He was grilled for days on everything from obscure legal facts designed to test his overall knowledge to questions about his past.

that was rattling the nation. They were also afraid that Marshall, being such a strong advocate for African Americans, would use his power to make things easier for those who were causing some of the trouble in the cities.

In the end, however, the senators who wanted to block Marshall's appointment to the Supreme Court were outnumbered, and he was given the position. Marshall said that he was "greatly honored by the appointment and its confirmation." He later added that he would be ". . . ever mindful of my obligation to the Constitution and to the goal of equal justice under law." Lyndon Johnson was thrilled. He believed Marshall would be a strong role model for younger African Americans. He hoped they would see Marshall's influential role in the United States as an indication that African Americans could effect changes that would improve their lives.

While it was not surprising that many whites were angered by Marshall's appointment, it must have come as a small shock to Johnson to find that a certain percentage of African Americans were angered too. Some felt that Marshall was being used as a symbolic tool by Lyndon Johnson to promote his image as a supporter of civil rights. Others added that Johnson may have given Marshall the appointment in order to assure more African American votes in the next presidential election.

Whether this was true will never be known, for Johnson did not run for president again. By the end of 1967, as his presidential term was coming to a close, racial tension in the United States was at an all-time high and the war in Vietnam, in which the United States was playing a large role, was not going well. Johnson decided it would be best if he left the presidency to someone else.

MARSHALL'S NEW ROLE

Meanwhile, Marshall settled into his new position. It kept him very busy, which left him less time to spend with his wife and sons. Although he wanted to be more involved in their lives, the demands of being a justice of the Supreme Court often kept him from doing so. Occasionally, if the boys had a baseball game or a school event, Marshall would send a friend or a trusted associate in his place.

The new Supreme Court, photographed in October of 1967, with Marshall at top right. The man directly in front of him, Justice William J. Brennan, Jr., shared almost all of Marshall's legal and political views and would become one of his dearest friends.

Justice Marshall took a decidedly liberal stance on most issues that came before him. He was compassionate and open-minded, usually making decisions that helped those who needed it most rather than giants such as large corporations or phenomenally wealthy individuals. When he began his tenure on the Supreme Court, the majority of the other eight justices also held liberal beliefs. As a result, Marshall often found the court's decisions were to his liking.

Much to Marshall's disappointment, this was to change fairly quickly. While he believed liberalism held the keys to the nation's health and progress, many of the U.S. voters didn't agree. Regardless of all the good work Lyndon Johnson had done concerning civil rights, the country was in a mess when Johnson's term as president drew to a close. Between the problems at home and the problems in Vietnam, most citizens were ready for a change in leadership.

The Republican Party's presidential candidate, Richard M. Nixon, knew this, and he knew how to make the most out of it. He promised to crack down on crime in the streets by sending out more police. He said he wanted to restore order to U.S. society. To the millions of people who were tired of all the violence and tension, Nixon's words sounded like beautiful music. Unsurprisingly, he won the election and became the nation's new president in 1968.

As president, Nixon had the power to appoint new justices to the Supreme Court. This worried Marshall because he believed Nixon would appoint the kind of people who weren't liberal-minded enough to be concerned about the welfare of minorities, poor people, and so on. Even worse, Marshall realized, was the fact that a number of the liberal justices on the Supreme Court would be retiring soon. They were getting older, and they didn't have the strength to perform their duties anymore. For Marshall, dark clouds were gathering overhead.

To be fair, Thurgood Marshall was never so liberal that he refused to even acknowledge the values of conservative thinking. He was a fair justice who believed in considering all points of view. For example, he believed one of the biggest reasons the people of the United States wanted the country to become more conservative was because they were tired of African American leaders who thought breaking the law and encouraging violence was the best way to gain equality. When Marshall fought segregation as a young lawyer, even those who didn't agree with him had to admit he was waging an honorable fight.

It was impossible for Marshall and those like him to admire people who strove to burn down buildings, loot stores, and gang up on defenseless white people. People like this were driven by a wild anger that was not tempered by reason or sense. It often drove them to do foolish, harmful things. What they didn't seem to understand—but Marshall knew all along—was that, by acting this way, they were hurting their cause rather than helping it.

ANOTHER SOLDIER FALLS

In July of 1974, Chief Justice Earl Warren died of a heart attack. He was a dear friend of Marshall's who had helped African Americans make huge strides toward equality. With Warren gone and other liberal justices being replaced by those of President Nixon's choosing, Marshall suddenly found himself part of the Supreme Court's liberal minority. The years ahead would not be easy for him. Nevertheless, he decided to stick it out and do the best he could. After all, it wasn't just his own interests that he had to protect—it was those of every African American who was hoping for a decent life in the United States.

There were times when the philosophical differences between the liberal justices and the conservative justices didn't seem to get in the way, and decisions based purely on fairness and common sense ruled the day. In 1969, the court was asked to make a decision on a case that was related to Marshall's famous *Brown* v. *Board of Education*, which forever abolished racial segregation in the nation's schools. In this new case, a group of students from Mississippi complained that the people who ran the schools in their area were taking too long to mix white students with African American students. School officials were putting off integration for as long as possible, using one excuse after another to avoid

Chief Justice Earl Warren, seen here with Marshall aboard the presidential yacht *Sequoia*, was that rarest of men. He was admired and respected both by liberals and conservatives. As governor of California, he championed progressive policies, increasing state services while lowering taxes.

obeying the law. All nine justices agreed, and they ordered that the Mississippi schools immediately permit students of all races to begin attending classes together.

There were other times when Marshall and the other liberal justices found themselves in total disagreement with their conservative colleagues. One of the clearest examples of this concerned the death penalty. Only the worst crimes can be punished by the death penalty. The most common crime to be punished by it is called first-degree murder, which involves the careful planning and killing of another person. Another crime punishable by death, which is less common than murder, is treason. Treason is a thought-out attempt by someone to destroy his or her own government.

Throughout his life, Marshall was against the death penalty, regardless of how horrible the crime that was committed. He felt it went against the part of the Constitution's Eighth Amendment that disallows "cruel and unusual punishment" in the United States. The more conservative-minded justices disagreed, believing that the death penalty was acceptable in some instances. It came up in a few cases during Marshall's time as a Supreme Court justice, and it was his hope that he would somehow find a way to abolish it. That hope was never realized, however.

Marshall looks on in October of 1977 while sculptor Reuben Kramer works on a bust of Marshall's head. The bust was commissioned in Baltimore to celebrate the achievements and impact of one of its most famous sons.

ELEVEN

The Final Years

In early July of 1976, Marshall suffered a mild heart attack. Earlier the same day, the court had made a final decision on a case related to the death penalty, which had not gone Marshall's way. Many who knew him could see that he had been emotionally shattered by the decision, and it was believed that the resulting stress had contributed to the attack. A lifetime of smoking, drinking, eating the wrong foods, rarely exercising, and working almost around the clock certainly didn't help his health, either. His wife and two sons would often nag him about his poor habits, but he wouldn't do much more than grumble in response.

In spite of his ill health, Marshall carried on as best he could. He would reduce his workload only to the point where it no longer endangered his health. But he had no intention of leaving his treasured position of influence in the highest court in the United States.

In time, Marshall would come to cherish this decision, for the conservative majority grew even larger, and he had to maintain a liberal voice on the court. In the 1980s, Republican president Ronald Reagan was called on to appoint three new justices to the Supreme Court. On the surface, it looked as if his choices were in fact quite liberal. One, Sandra Day O'Connor, was the first woman ever to hold a place on the Supreme Court. The other, Antonin Scalia, was the first justice of Italian descent. However, both were very conservative in their viewpoints.

HANGING IN THERE

With his power in the Supreme Court diminishing, it would have been easy for Marshall to give up. But many of the people who worked closely with him at the time say that nothing of the sort happened. Instead, he was just as cheerful and humorous as ever. He had to become

Proud Father

Thurgood Marshall's two sons, Thurgood, Jr. and John, went on to have distinguished careers that made their father very proud. Thurgood, Jr. became a lawyer like his father, eventually working for the Supreme Court Historical Society and, from 1997 to 2001, as assistant to the president and secretary to the cabinet under President William Jefferson Clinton. His brother, John, went into law enforcement and, in February of 2000, made history when he became the first African American to head of the U.S. Marshals Service.

something of a hustler and a dealmaker now that he was so overwhelmingly outnumbered on the court. He had to find new and creative ways to get his fellow justices to understand his points of view. He also spent time lecturing to scores of young people, encouraging them to take up the never-ending fight for equal rights of all minorities living in the United States. He told them not to give up hope.

It is possible that Marshall decided to retire when his last liberal friend on the Supreme Court, William Brennan, resigned in July of 1990. Brennan's health had been failing for some time. He tried to hang on for as long as he could, but eventually he had to let go. "There's nobody here that can persuade the way Brennan can persuade," Marshall said during a television interview that same year. He said that Brennan ". . . cannot be replaced."

After Brennan's retirement, Marshall was all alone, a devoted liberal working against a legion of conservatives. The president at the time,

An Age of Advancement

The 1990s saw rapid growth in the field of technology, especially computer technology. Suddenly, every home seemed to have a personal computer. The 1990s also saw historic strides for minorities in the United States. William Jefferson Clinton, president from 1992 to 2000, created millions of new jobs, many of which were filled by African Americans. Clinton also fought to make it easier for African American business owners to get bank loans. He gave tax breaks to the poorest African Americans and created government programs that enabled lower-income African American families to buy their own home.

George Herbert Walker Bush, appointed another conservative, David Souter, to replace Brennan. Now, the odds were all but insurmountable. So, in June of 1991, Marshall announced that he, too, would retire. Eventually Bush would replaced him with another African American, Clarence Thomas, who was a conservative.

THE DEATH OF A GREAT WARRIOR

Marshall continued to speak to large audiences, reminding them that while African Americans had made great progress in the twentieth century, their fight for equality was far from over. "The battle has not been won. We have barely begun," he once told a crowd that included both African Americans and whites. "Our futures are bound together." He passionately tried to imprint some sense of the past on his younger listeners, many of whom had never been denied a job, a meal, or a seat on a bus simply because they were born with dark skin. Eventually, Marshall's declining health caught up with him, culminating in massive heart failure that took his life on January 24, 1993. On that day, one of the greatest soldiers in the long fight for equal rights for African Americans died.

Perhaps Marshall's most memorable achievement was the pivotal role he played in overturning the ruling from the dreadful 1896 *Plessy* v. *Ferguson* case, which basically condemned African Americans to decades of segregation and second-class citizenship. Thanks to his tireless work on *Brown* v. *Board of Education*, millions of African Americans now enjoy the same educational rights and opportunities as whites.

As an attorney for the NAACP, he struck fear in the hearts of those who were keeping segregationist practices alive, especially in America's Deep South. Where once there was a time when these people could manifest their racist attitudes with impunity, they now suddenly found themselves faced with a formidable foe in Thurgood Marshall—a man who permitted no argument or negotiation when it came to the proper treatment of African Americans. He also enhanced and improved the NAACP's stature and respectability, making it a point of pride for millions while boldly augmenting its power base in the southern United States; a task that was long overdue.

With his appointment and subsequent confirmation to the Supreme Court, he inspired countless young African Americans to believe in themselves and in their dreams. He proved that it was possible for minorities to reach great heights and wield true power. From his seat on the most influential bench in the land, he passed down judgments and wrote opinions that championed the rights of the poor, the oppressed, the downtrodden, and all others who had been cast aside by the many injustices of U.S. society. Even from a lofty position that allowed him to rub elbows with the wealthiest and most powerful people in the world, Marshall could still relate to the common person—the one who had to get up early each day, put in long hours of hard work, and come home with little to show for it. Marshall never forgot his roots, and he used his clout as a Supreme Court justice to fight for the people who continued to struggle as he had.

In the end, it is possible that Thurgood Marshall's most lasting legacy will be the simple concept that people who have been wronged must fight for what they believe and for what is right. Thurgood Marshall was a fighter, first and foremost, willing to devote his life to breaking down outmoded ideas that had prevented African Americans from having opportunities to which they were fully entitled. He proved that the struggle was worthwhile and that, if you carried on the crusade long enough, your efforts would be rewarded.

Democratic president William Jefferson Clinton and his wife Hillary Rodham Clinton (who would later become a New York senator) offer their condolences to Cissy Marshall two days after her husband's death. Clinton appointed dozens of African Americans and other minorities to high government posts.

Timeline

1908 Thurgood Marshall is born in Baltimore, Maryland, the second son of William and Norma Marshall.

1914 Marshall begins first grade in a segregated Baltimore elementary school.

World War I begins.

1917 The United States enters World War I.

1918 World War I ends.

1921 Marshall begins ninth grade at the segregated Colored High and Training School.

1925 Marshall begins his college years at Lincoln University, an all-African American institution, in Pennsylvania.

1929 On October 29, the U.S. stock market crashes. It is the beginning of the Great Depression.

1930 Marshall graduates from Lincoln University with honors.

1930 Marshall applies for enrollment at the University of Maryland's law school, but is denied admission because he is African American. He then applies to Howard University's law school and is accepted.

1933 Marshall graduates first in his class from Howard University School of Law.

1934 Marshall sues the University of Maryland for refusing to admit Donald Murray, an African-American, to its law school. A year later, Marshall wins the lawsuit.

1935 Marshall leaves Baltimore to move to Harlem in New York City, to work for the National Association for the Advancement of Colored People (NAACP).

1938 Marshall becomes chief legal counsel for the NAACP.

1939 World War II breaks out in Europe and Asia.

1941 The United States becomes involved in World War II.

1945 World War II ends.

1948 President Harry S. Truman signs a law forbidding the unequal treatment of African Americans in all U.S. government jobs, including the military.

1950 Harry and Liza Briggs file a lawsuit against the state of South Carolina because they feel their son's school, which is for African Americans only, is not as good as the schools for white children. Marshall soon gets involved in the case.

1951 Marshall moves the Briggs case to the U.S. Supreme Court.

1952 The Briggs case, now called *Brown* v. *Board of Education,* begins in the U.S. Supreme Court, on December 9.

1954 On May 17, the U.S. Supreme Court decided in favor of Marshall and his clients, and school segregation in America was legally abolished.

Marshall's first wife, Vivian, dies after a long battle with cancer.

Marshall marries Cecilia Suyat.

1960 The United States elects a new president, Democrat John F. Kennedy. Kennedy is a champion of civil rights, who is committed to helping African Americans in their fight for equal rights.

1963 President Kennedy is assassinated in Dallas, Texas, on November 22. He is succeeded by Vice President Lyndon Baines Johnson.

1964 President Johnson approves and signs the Civil Rights Act, guaranteeing African Americans numerous rights and privileges they had sought for decades.

1965 President Johnson appoints Marshall as the U.S. solicitor general. Marshall is the first African American to hold that position.

1965 United States's involvement in the Vietnam War begins to increase. More U.S. troops are sent into the region to take part in the fighting.

1967 President Johnson nominates Marshall to be the first African American justice on the Supreme Court.

1968 The war in Vietnam is not going well. Many Americans want the United States out of the conflict. Richard M. Nixon, promising to do this, wins the election to become the nation's next president.

1973 The last U.S. troops leave Vietnam.

1974 Embroiled in a scandal, Richard M. Nixon resigns the presidency.

1976 In July, Marshall has a mild heart attack. He recovers and continues working.

1990 William Brennan, the only other liberal judge besides Marshall on the Supreme Court, resigns his position due to failing health.

1991 In June, Marshall announces that he will retire from the U.S. Supreme Court.

1993 Thurgood Marshall dies of heart failure on January 24.

To Find Out More

BOOKS

Adler, David A. *A Picture Book of Thurgood Marshall*. New York: Holiday House, 1999.

Dunham, Montrew. *Thurgood Marshall: Young Justice*. New York: Aladdin Library, 1998.

Gibson, Karen Bush. *Thurgood Marshall: A Photo-Illustrated Biography*. Mankato, MN: Bridgestone Books, 2002.

Kent, Deborah. *Thurgood Marshall and the Supreme Court*. Danbury, CT: Children's Press, 1997.

McLeese, Don. *Thurgood Marshall*. Vero Beach, FL: Rourke Book Company, Inc., 2002.

Rowh, Mark. *Thurgood Marshall: Civil Rights Attorney and Supreme Court Justice*. Berkeley Heights, NJ: Enslow Publishers, Inc., 2002.

Whitelaw, Nancy. *Mr. Civil Rights: The Story of Thurgood Marshall*. Greensboro, NC: Morgan Reynolds, 2002.

Williams, Carla. *Thurgood Marshall*. Chanhassen, MN: Child's World, 2002.

ORGANIZATIONS AND ONLINE SITES

African American History
http://www.lib.washington.edu/subject/History/tm/black.html

This page offers dozens of links to topics concerning nearly every aspect of African American history in the United States.

Howard University School of Law
http://www.law.howard.edu

This is the site of the school from which Thurgood Marshall received his law degree.

The National Association for the Advancement of Colored People
http://www.naacp.org/

This is the NAACP's official Web site. It contains information on the association's history, membership, leadership, local branches, and extensive programs. It also includes links to *The Crisis* magazine, which was started by the NAACP in 1910.

Supreme Court Basics
http://www.infoplease.com/ce6/history/A0847276.html

This site has basic information on the Supreme Court and its purpose, history, and daily functions. It also includes a detailed bibliography and information on individual justices, both past and present.

The Supreme Court of the United States
http://www.supremecourtus.gov/

This is the official site for the United States Supreme Court. It offers information on current cases as well as visiting hours for the public.

Thurgood Marshall, American Revolutionary
http://www.thurgoodmarshall.com

This site is based on Juan Williams's book *Thurgood Marshall: American Revolutionary*. The book is written for adults, but the site has excellent features for every age group, including interviews with Marshall, some of his speeches, and an excellent photo gallery.

The Thurgood Marshall Scholarship Fund
http://www.thurgoodmarhsallfund.org

This site contains information about the Thurgood Marshall Scholarship Fund, which was created in 1987 (with the help of Marshall himself) to assist in the cost of advanced education for African American students.

We Shall Overcome—*Brown v. Board of Education*
http://www.cr.nps.gov/NR/travel/civilrights/ka1.htm

Called the "*Brown* v. *Board of Education* National Historic Site," this site gives an overview of the amazing events of Marshall's most famous case, as well as details about the other people involved and how they went about reaching the decision that changed the United States forever.

A Note on Sources

Many books and articles have already been written about the amazing life of Thurgood Marshall, and it has been a privilege to contribute to that list. Marshall may have spent most of his time in the very "adult" world of courtrooms, conference rooms, and law offices, but he was there fighting for the principles of fairness and equality, which people of any age can appreciate.

Because he accomplished so much and became such a celebrated figure, I had plenty of material from which to work. Two of the most useful books were Davis and Clark's *Thurgood Marshall: Warrior at the Bar, Rebel on the Bench* and Juan Williams's *Thurgood Marshall: American Revolutionary*. Both were well written and followed a sensible chronology, making them easy to use as references. I also turned to Microsoft's Encarta encyclopedia for basic information on key historical events such as the Great Depression and the Vietnam War.

Online sites about Marshall were too numerous to count, but I did manage to streamline my personal list. I was able to locate the official decision from the Supreme Court concerning *Brown* v. *Board of Education*, written by Chief Justice Earl Warren. It contained lots of technical legal language, but after sifting through it and getting down to the meaning of the Court's opinion—that segregation had no place in U.S. society—my spine tingled. I couldn't help but wonder what was going through Warren's mind when the words flowed out of him all those years ago. Did he realize, with that one document, how he was changing the world?

It was a great pleasure to write and research this book. I hope you get an equal amount of enjoyment and education out of reading it.

—*Wil Mara*

Index

About the Author

Wil Mara has been writing since the 1980s and has more than sixty books to his credit. Most of his early works were non-fiction titles about animals. In the early 1990s, he turned to fiction, ghostwriting three of the popular Boxcar Children Mysteries. He has since published four other novels, a handful of short stories, and numerous early-reader biographies for Scholastic Library Publishing. He lives with his wife and three daughters in northern New Jersey.